Please visit our website, www.garethstevens.com. For a free color catalog of all our high-quality books, call toll free 1-800-542-2595 or fax 1-877-542-2596.

Library of Congress Cataloging-in-Publication Data
Names: Seeley, M. H., author.
Title: 20 fun facts about Alexander Hamilton / M H Seeley.
Other titles: Twenty fun facts about Alexander Hamilton
Description: New York : Gareth Stevens, [2018] | Series: Fun fact file:
  founding fathers | Includes index.
Identifiers: LCCN 2016057416| ISBN 9781538202883 (pbk. book) | ISBN
  9781538202708 (6 pack) | ISBN 9781538202821 (library bound book)
Subjects: LCSH: Hamilton, Alexander, 1757-1804–Juvenile literature. |
  Statesmen–United States–Biography–Juvenile literature. | United
  States–Politics and government–1783-1809–Juvenile literature.
Classification: LCC E302.6.H2 S274 2018 | DDC 973.4092 [B] –dc23
LC record available at https://lccn.loc.gov/2016057416

First Edition

Published in 2018 by
Gareth Stevens Publishing
111 East 14th Street, Suite 349
New York, NY 10003

Designer: Sam DeMartin
Editor: Ryan Nagelhout

Photo credits: Cover, p. 1 (portrait) Everett - Art/Shutterstock.com; cover, p. 1 (background) Ed
Vebell/Archive Photos/Getty Images; pp. 5, 10 (Madison) Muboshgu/Wikimedia Commons;
p. 6 Rainer Lesniewski/Shutterstock.com; p. 7 Carlos andre Santos/Shutterstock.com; p. 8 Dfarrell07/
Wikimedia Commons; p. 9 Dal89/Wikimedia Commons; p. 10 (Jay) Scewing/Wikimedia Commons;
p. 11 Elisfkc/Wikimedia Commons; p. 12 Krscal/Wikimedia Commons; p. 13 DEA PICTURE LIBRARY/
Getty Images; p. 14 Davepape/Wikimedia Commons; p. 15 Illegitimate Barrister/Wikimedia Commons;
p. 16 Futurist110/Wikimedia Commons; p. 17 (both) AlexLMX/Shutterstock.com; p. 18 Godot13/
Wikimedia Commons; p. 19 Norman Chan/Shutterstock.com; pp. 20, 22, 23 courtesy of the Library of
Congress; p. 21 J. Helgason/Shutterstock.com; p. 24 Fœ/Wikimedia Commons; p. 25 Billy Hathorn/
Wikimedia Commons; p. 26 Jim.henderson/Wikimedia Commons; p. 27 SWHAarchivist1/Wikimedia
Commons; p. 29 Zack Frank/Shutterstock.com.

Printed in China

CPSIA compliance information: Batch #CS17GS: For further information contact Gareth Stevens, New York, New York at 1-800-542-2595.

Contents

The Forgotten Founder. 4

Family Ties. 6

Show It, Poet 8

Writings on the Wall. 10

By George!. 12

Military Might. 14

Unfriendly Founding Fathers 16

Money, Money, Money. 18

All Press Is Good Press 20

Burr and Jefferson 22

The Duels. 24

Family Loss 26

An Uncertain Legacy 28

Glossary. 30

For More Information. 31

Index 32

Words in the glossary appear in **bold** type the first time they are used in the text.

The Forgotten Founder

For a long time, Alexander Hamilton was a largely forgotten Founding Father. Despite the many things he did for America, Hamilton's name is often missing from stories starring the likes of George Washington, Thomas Jefferson, John Adams, and Benjamin Franklin. In many ways, this is Hamilton's own fault—he wrote down many of his worst mistakes for all to see!

Recently, however, Americans have taken a second look at Hamilton and his important place in early American history. Let's learn some more about this Founding Father!

Alexander Hamilton was born
on an island in the Caribbean
Sea, but became an important
part of early American history.

FACT 1

Hamilton didn't know his own birth year!

It's either 1755 or 1757, but no one can be sure! Hamilton was born on Nevis, a tiny island in the Caribbean Sea. His father was a Scottish trader, and his mother was a Frenchwoman.

CARIBBEAN SEA

Sandy
Point Town

△ Mt. Liamuiga

SAINT KITTS

BASSETERRE
☆

Great
Salt
Pond

The Narrows

CARIBBEAN
SEA

NEVIS

Charlestown

△ Nevis Peak

When Hamilton was a boy, his family moved to the island of St. Croix.

An apprentice is someone who learns a job from a person who has done that job for a long time.

Hamilton grew up without a father.

Hamilton's father, a failed businessman, deserted his family when Alexander was young. His mother, Rachel, supported Alexander and his brother by running a small shop until she died when Hamilton was about 12.

After Hamilton's mother died and Hamilton went to America to study, his older brother remained in St. Croix. Little is known about him, though at one point he was apprenticed to a carpenter.

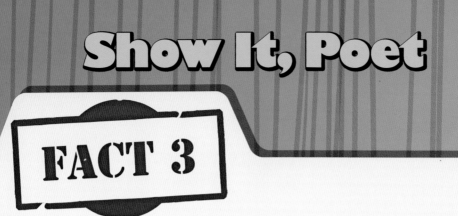

FACT 3

Hamilton was such a good writer that he received a free education.

In 1772, teenage Hamilton wrote to his father telling about a hurricane that had hit St. Croix. The letter later appeared in the *Royal Danish American Gazette*. Readers found it so beautiful they collected money to send the young writer to America for an education.

Hamilton traveled to New York City, where he kept writing and attended school.

Hamilton was an excellent poet, though he often published under a fake name.

Hamilton wrote all the time! He wrote letters, long papers called essays, articles, and even poems. He once wrote a poem for his wife that was so beautiful she put it in a little bag and wore it around her neck!

Elizabeth Hamilton

Elizabeth Hamilton, Alexander's wife, was from a wealthy and important New York family—the Schuylers.

FACT 5

Hamilton wrote 52 of the 85 articles in *The Federalist Papers*.

When the Constitution was first written, Hamilton, James Madison, and John Jay got together to write articles trying to make voters think it should be passed. They were supposed to split up the articles, but Jay got sick, and Hamilton wrote most of them!

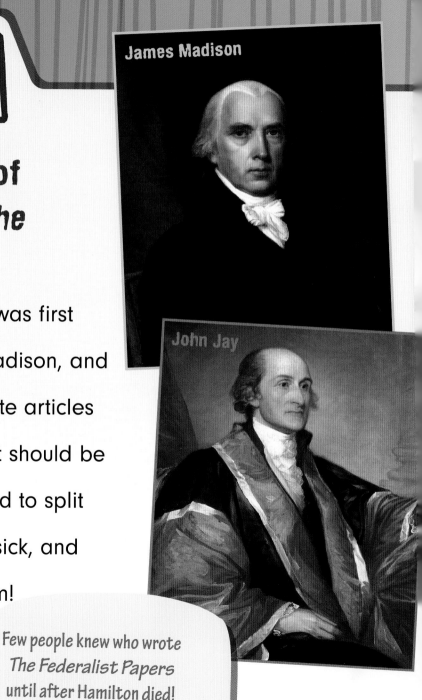

James Madison

John Jay

Few people knew who wrote *The Federalist Papers* until after Hamilton died!

Hamilton's writings ruined one Founding Father's chance of becoming president—his own!

Hamilton often wrote about things that got him into trouble, including his famous *Observations on Certain Documents*. He did this in order to clear himself of worse charges—that he'd been part of a questionable financial plan. But what he wrote about hurt his **reputation** a great deal!

OBSERVATIONS

ON

CERTAIN DOCUMENTS

CONTAINED IN NO. V & VI OF

"THE HISTORY OF THE UNITED STATES
FOR THE YEAR 1796,"

IN WHICH THE

CHARGE OF SPECULATION

AGAINST

ALEXANDER HAMILTON,

LATE SECRETARY OF THE TREASURY,

IS FULLY REFUTED.

WRITTEN BY HIMSELF.

PHILADELPHIA:

PRINTED FOR JOHN FENNO, BY JOHN BIOREN,
1797.

Hamilton cleared his name of illegal activity, but did great harm to himself along the way. He would never run for president or hold public office again.

By George!

FACT 7

Hamilton and Washington had a fight so bad they didn't speak to one another for a long time.

Hamilton became Washington's aide during the American Revolution. But after 4 years, they had an argument: Washington yelled at Hamilton for being late and—his pride hurt—Hamilton quit. Washington said he was sorry, but Hamilton didn't accept it. Their friendship was uneasy for many years.

George Washington

Washington and Hamilton were close for many years, but their friendship, like most of the Founding Fathers' friendships, had its troubles.

George Washington's funeral procession

The last letter Washington wrote before he died was to Hamilton.

Despite their long fight, Hamilton and Washington became very close during Washington's presidency. Hamilton once wrote that Washington was "**essential** to me," and Washington's very last letter was to Hamilton. It was in support of Hamilton's wish to create a national military **academy**.

When George Washington died, the whole country was sad, especially Hamilton.

FACT 9

Hamilton's army unit is still in action today.

In 1776, Hamilton was made captain of the 1st Battalion, 5th Field Artillery Unit in New York. Today, that unit is the oldest one still operating in the US Army. It's also the only one left that fought in the American Revolution!

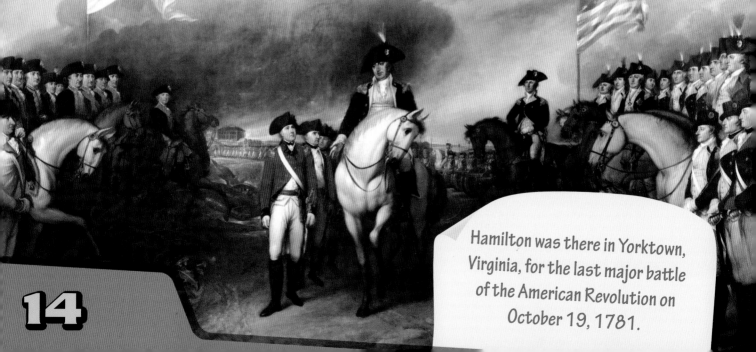

Hamilton was there in Yorktown, Virginia, for the last major battle of the American Revolution on October 19, 1781.

Hamilton created the US Coast Guard!

In 1789, Hamilton suggested boats police the American coastline to guard businesses from illegal trading. Hamilton created the Revenue Cutter Service (RCS) in 1790 to police the American coastline to make sure nobody was trading illegally. Today, it's called the US Coast Guard!

Smuggling was a huge issue at that time, and the RCS made sure that no **contraband** made it to American shores.

FACT 11

Hamilton and Thomas Jefferson hated one another.

Jefferson thought the central government should be weak, which would let each state decide how to govern. Hamilton, however, thought the central government should have more power. Jefferson thought Hamilton's ideas about banking gave the government too much power.

◀ Thomas Jefferson

JEFFERSON

limited national government; share power with states

fear of dictator rule

strict interpretation of Constitution

national bank unconstitional

farming-based economy

often supported by farmers and tradespeople

HAMILTON

power concentrated in federal government

fear of mob rule

loose interpretation of Constitution

national bank constitutional

manufacturing-based economy

often supported by lawyers, investors, clergy, merchants, manufacturerers

17

FACT 12

Hamilton was the very first secretary of the treasury and created America's very first national bank!

Hamilton knew that running a country costs a lot of money, and the national government would need some way to oversee it. So in spite of a lot of objections from other politicians, Hamilton created the First Bank of the United States.

This check, signed by John Astor from the Bank of the United States, is one of the earliest in American history!

WHO'S ON THE
MONEY?

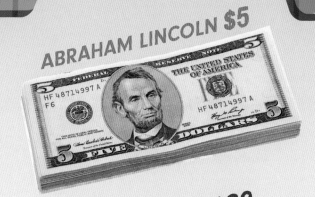

ABRAHAM LINCOLN $5

GEORGE WASHINGTON $1

ANDREW JACKSON $20

ALEXANDER HAMILTON $10

BENJAMIN FRANKLIN $100

ULYSSES S. GRANT $50

Many Founding Fathers found their way onto our money. Lincoln, Washington, Franklin, and Hamilton all helped start the United States of America.

FACT 13

Hamilton started America's longest-running newspaper.

Lots of Hamilton's creations stuck around. The *New York Post* was a way for Hamilton to publish his many opinions on a wide range of topics. Hamilton used to speak his **editorials** out loud to someone who wrote them down. No rewrites!

Hamilton formed *The New York Post* in 1801 with the name *New-York Evening Post*.

Editorial from the New York Evening Post
April 24, 1908.
LEGISLATURE, GOVERNOR AND PEOPLE.

Why did the Legislature of the State of New York adjourn yesterday with open insults to the Governor? Had any member a grievance against him which could be publicly stated? The most embittered Assemblyman could not allege that Gov. Hughes has not been absolutely honest. The most drunken Tammany Senator could not assert that he has not been unusually laborious, conscientious to a degree, patient and courteous; nor that he has brought to his work great ability and lofty personal standards.

He has not attempted to cheat or bully the Legislature. He has neither bargained nor log-rolled; has not used his veto power, or the threat of it, to terrorize legislators, nor trafficked in patronage to buy their votes. Furthermore, it is admitted by all impartial observers, outside the State as well as in it, that Gov. Hughes has won a reputation and conquered an admiration not equalled by any Governor of New York since Tilden and Cleveland. What then is the explanation of the strong dislike, running hard upon hatred, which the Legislature exhibits for Gov. Hughes?

Putting minor reasons one side, the chief one is that the Governor has endeavored to hold the Legislature to its duty. He has sought to make it in fact, what it is in theory, truly representative of the whole people. What he had to face was a set of men too many of whom were "owned" by bosses like Barnes of Albany. Others were too narrow-minded, too tied down to the petty concerns of locality, to consider fairly the large interests of the State. Broad and sound public policy meant little to them, compared with the exigent demands of politicians whom they feared, or powerful men whom they courted. And the secret of their rage at the Governor is that he has not only stood for the people in general, but has gone out into the district and proved that many legislators were misrepresenting their particular constituencies. Talk about Mr. Hughes's usurpation of power is childish. It is the others who have usurped power. Will any man stand up and say Boss Barnes has any right to pose as the dictator of Albany County?

He has filched his authority. The voice of the decent people--and they are in the vast majority--has been overwhelmingly declared against him. Hence it is that Gov. Hughes in going direct to the people as he has done, and as he will do still more freely in the next two weeks, is merely seeking to make our institutions truly representative, and to make them work for the common good.

One place where Hamilton did *not* use a fake name was on the US Constitution, which he signed.

FACT 14

Hamilton often published his opinion pieces under a pseudonym, or fake name.

In Hamilton's day, writing the wrong thing in a newspaper could have seriously bad **consequences**. He also wrote poetry and his parts of *The Federalist Papers* under the pseudonym "Publius."

FACT 15

Hamilton and Aaron Burr once solved a murder together.

Hamilton and Burr had a messy friendship. The pair worked together on the first murder trial in US history. They defended Levi Weeks, a New York City man who was thought to have killed a young woman. Together, they won the case!

REPORT

OF THE

T R I A L

OF

LEVI WEEKS,

On an Indictment for the Murder

OF GULIELMA SANDS,

ON MONDAY THE THIRTY-FIRST DAY OF MARCH, AND TUESDAY THE FIRST DAY OF APRIL, 1807.

TAKEN IN SHORT HAND BY THE CLERK OF THE COURT

NEW-YORK:
PRINTED BY JOHN FURMAN,
AND SOLD AT HIS BLANK, STAMP & STATIONARY SHOP,
OPPOSITE THE CITY HALL.
1800.

Elma Sands was found dead in a well just outside New York City. Hamilton and Burr worked together to prove Levi Weeks didn't kill her.

A.Burr

Despite their hatred for one another, Hamilton helped Jefferson get elected president in 1800!

Jefferson and Burr were tied in the vote that decided who became the country's third president. Hamilton, who disagreed with almost everything Jefferson thought, told people in his Federalist political party to vote for Jefferson. He thought Jefferson would make a better president than Burr.

Burr became vice president in the election of 1800 but never forgave Hamilton for not supporting him against Jefferson.

FACT 17

Hamilton might have lost his famous and deadly duel with Aaron Burr on purpose!

As he lay dying from Burr's bullet, Hamilton said he tried to miss Burr with his shot on purpose—in other words, he planned to lose the duel! Whether or not that's true, Hamilton was shot, and Burr was not.

Burr and Hamilton dueled because the two exchanged insults in a series of letters in 1804. But they had disagreed about many things over many years.

24

Hamilton's oldest son, Phillip, died in a duel in the same spot where Burr shot Hamilton!

Hamilton's famous duel took place in Weehawken, New Jersey, across the Hudson River from New York City. It's the same spot where his son, Phillip, had died years earlier. Phillip tried to defend his father's honor in a duel in 1801.

THE
HAMILTON · BURR DUEL
JULY 11, 1804

The most famous duel in American history took place on this date at the dueling grounds in Weehawken, between political rivals, General Alexander Hamilton and sitting Vice-President of the United States, Colonel Aaron Burr. Hamilton fell, mortally wounded, and died the next day in New York City. Tragically, Hamilton's son Philip had also met his death here in a duel in 1801.

Dedicated on July 11, 2004, the 200th Anniversary of the Duel.

Phillip Hamilton dueled George Eacker after Eacker spoke poorly of Alexander Hamilton in a speech.

FACT 19

When the Hamiltons lost Phillip, they lost their daughter Angelica, too.

Angelica, a year younger than Phillip, was beautiful, gifted, and well liked. But her brother's death came as such a shock that her mental health suffered and she never became well again. She died in a mental hospital at age 73.

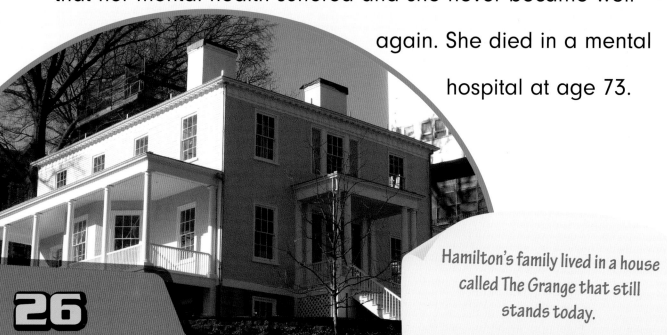

Hamilton's family lived in a house called The Grange that still stands today.

After his death, Hamilton's wife Elizabeth created New York's first private orphanage to honor her husband.

Elizabeth created the Orphan Asylum Society in 1806. She was its director and vice president for many years. The group still works with children today, though it is now called Graham Windham. Elizabeth outlived Alexander by 50 years!

The Orphan Asylum Society housed and educated orphans in New York City.

An Uncertain Legacy

Alexander Hamilton was a man ahead of his time. So many of his ideas and inventions are still in use today. His Bank of New York is the second oldest in the country. You can still buy a copy of his *New York Post*, and the coast guard still operates today. In fact, it still used the **communication** guides he wrote until 1962!

People are more interested in Alexander Hamilton than ever! There's even a musical about his life. His **legacy** continues to change, hundreds of years after he died.

29

Glossary

academy: a school used for special training for a certain skill

communication: having to do with the act or method of sharing thoughts, opinions, or ideas

consequence: the result of an action

contraband: items that are not allowed

duel: a fight with deadly weapons between two people, with witnesses present, because of a wrong done by one to the other

editorial: a newspaper or magazine article that is based only on opinion

essential: necessary

legacy: something that is passed down from someone

orphanage: a home for children who no longer have parents to care for them

reputation: the views that are held about something or someone

smuggling: the act of sneaking in something that is not allowed

For More Information

Books

Burgan, Michael. *Soldier and Founder: Alexander Hamilton*. Minneapolis, MN: Compass Point Books, 2009.

Fritz, Jean. *Alexander Hamilton: The Outsider*. New York, NY: G.P. Putnam's Sons, 2011.

St. George, Judith. *The Duel: The Parallel Lives of Alexander Hamilton & Aaron Burr*. New York, NY: Viking, 2009.

Websites

The Alexander Hamilton Awareness Society
the-aha-society.com
Find out more about Hamilton and his role in early America on the official AHA Society site.

Founders Online
founders.archives.gov
See Hamilton's actual writings and papers on this great site.

Hamilton and the US Constitution
pbs.org/wgbh/amex/duel/sfeature/hamiltonusconstituion.html
Learn all about Hamilton's role in creating the US Constitution.

Index

American Revolution 12, 14

articles 9, 10

Burr, Aaron 22, 23, 24

Caribbean Sea 5, 6

duel 24, 25

education 8

Federalist Papers, The 10, 21

First Bank of the United States 18, 28

Franklin, Benjamin 4, 19

Hamilton, Angelica 26

Hamilton, Elizabeth 9, 27

Hamilton, Phillip 25, 26

Jefferson, Thomas 4, 16, 17, 23

national military academy 13

Nevis 6, 8

New York City 8, 22, 25, 27

New York Post 20, 28

Observations on Certain Documents 11

Orphan Asylum Society 27

poems 9

Revenue Cutter Service 15

St. Croix 6, 7, 8

US Coast Guard 15, 28

Washington, George 4, 12, 13